Houseplant Hookups

For my mother, aunt, grandmothers,
(NYC) plant community, botanical book clurb . . . and lover(s),
and Cosmo and Miso, even though they can't read —A.I.

To my husband Matthew Smith.
Without your constant support and optimism, my
illustrations would never come to life in the way they do.
Thank you for all the late nights, home-cooked meals, and
for always helping to keep me caffeinated! —M.L.D.

First Edition
26 25 24 23   5 4 3 2 1

Text © 2023 Agatha Isabel
Illustrations © 2023 Mai Ly Degnan

Published by Gibbs Smith P.O. Box 667
Layton, Utah 84041
1.800.835.4993 orders www.gibbs-smith.com

Art director: Ryan Thomann
Editor: Gleni Bartels
Production designer: Virginia Snow
Production editor: Sue Collier
Production manager: Felix Gregorio

Printed and bound in Dongguan, China, by RR Donnelley Asia Printing Solutions
Gibbs Smith books are printed on either recycled, 100% post-consumer waste,
FSC-certified papers or on paper produced from sustainable PEFC-certified
forest/controlled wood source. Learn more at www.pefc.org.

Library of Congress Control Number: 2023936330

ISBN: 978-1-4236-6346-1

Houseplant Hookups

All the Dirt You Need to Find the Perfect Match

AGATHA ISABEL ILLUSTRATED BY **MAI LY DEGNAN**

Gibbs Smith

Contents

It Takes a Village . . . and a Garden

When I told people I was writing a book about plants told through dating profiles their eyes lit up, but they were a bit confused, too. *What do plants and dating have in common?* Well, lots. Like all potential romantic love matches, each potential plant match has its own personality, its own love language, its own list of #RelationshipGoals. And just like that person you met for drinks last week, it might take some time to figure out if you'll be able to grow and thrive together.

So who am I to write this book? I am a community-based, plant-loving, bad b*itch. And when it comes to dating, well, I'm a lover, not a fighter—a Gemini, with a Pisces moon and Taurus rising, to be exact. If you were to ask me when my love affair with plants began, I wouldn't be able pinpoint an exact moment. It's always been a part of me, nurtured by the women in my life. This matriarchal influence is summed up in my tattoo—a tulip, a rose, and a hibiscus with three circles—that reminds me of the three generations of plant-loving women, which include my mother, aunt, grandmother, and great-aunt, who all took turns planting and cultivating the garden that is me—in addition to teaching me how to keep plants alive.

And from there, I've grown a pretty decent garden in a couple different contexts. There's the literal sense, which you can see all over my social media, that has gotten me interviewed as a plant authority by places like the Spruce, Repeller, Apartment

Therapy, and CNN. (Maybe you've seen the tour of my 400+ plants that are inspired by my travels on YouTube?) And then there's the more figurative sense of a garden—growing a community that you care for and watch flourish. I found my initial plant community in Brooklyn, where I started an online store called Plant Ma Shop out of my apartment when I was furloughed during the pandemic. With my dearest plant pals, I started the nonprofit Planting for Progress, where I propagated some of my most special plants to raise funds for local nonprofits and communities during the times when they needed support the most.

So not only do I hope this book can show you that there's a perfect plant partner out there for everyone (yes, even you—just because you've killed the unkillable snake plant doesn't mean there's no hope!), but I also want to encourage you to get your hands dirty and get involved with cultivating and growing your community.

Agatha

It's easy to fall in love with a plant—but how do you make it love you back?

It might seem overwhelming, but you don't have to get caught in the weeds. This book approaches plant care like modern dating. You'll find out how to choose a partner that's right for you, where to find them, and what happens when they come home with you. You'll learn how to start a loving relationship and watch it grow—literally.

There are also 35 "dating profiles" for you to leaf through, which highlight the most attractive features, toxic traits, and essential info about the most common and most desirable plants. The dating range focuses on houseplants, which are grown indoors and typically kept in a home or office. No matter who you are or where you live, there's a planty partner that's right for you!

Let's dig up the dirt on houseplants.

Are You Ready to Put Yourself Out There?

When you're bringing something new into your life—whether it's a person or a plant—you should be realistic about each other's needs. To save yourself from heartbreak, it helps to be prepared before you commit to anything. With greenery, the first thing you should do is evaluate your space and get to know the basics of plant care. Here are some things to consider before taking the plunge into plant-based relationships.

GETTING INTO THE MOOD

When you're picking a date spot with a person, you might think about romantically dim lighting, background music, and general ambience. When you're picking a plant, think about your space. How's the lighting, general humidity, and vibe? What's your bachelor/ette pad like? Be honest with yourself.

You might get turned on by a big and "hole-y" monstera (page 37), but do you really have the room for a sprawling plant like that? If the answer is no, then maybe you can find love with a potted jade plant (page 57) that's small enough to sit on a windowsill—relationships are all about compromise! Be realistic about your lifestyle, too. Are you a nurturer? Then a polka dot begonia (page 82) that needs a lot of attention, might be your perfect match. Are you busy and unable to commit to consistent care? Look for a low-maintenance plant

like the ZZ plant (page 98) or snake plant (page 34) that only needs occasional watering.

GETTING LIT

Lighting is one of the most important things to keep in mind when choosing your houseplants. The amount of light your space receives depends on where you live, the time of year, how different your seasons are, and the direction your windows face.

Windows that face north only receive indirect light and are best for low-light plants. East-facing windows get bright light in the morning when the sun rises, then indirect light for the rest of the day. Plants that need low to moderate light are good for eastern exposure, especially those that like bright light but not a full-on sunshine assault. White walls, mirrors, and grow lights are ways to improve your lighting conditions and increase the range of plants you can keep.

Southern and western exposure provides the brightest, strongest light. Plants with higher light needs thrive in these sunny conditions. Blinds and sheer curtains can help diffuse this light, though, if you're considering a plant that shies away from the spotlight.

The bottom line: Plants will light up your life and give your space a glow up if you take time to understand your lighting situation!

GETTING HOT (OR COLD)

Obviously, sunlight is crucial for plants to grow so they can get that (vitamin) D, but it's maybe not so obvious that temperature must also be kept in mind. When plants grow in the wild, this balance is usually in harmony as they are in their endemic or more natural environment—when the light is more intense, the temperature and humidity might also rise. But most homes and offices are climate-controlled for our human needs. In winter, for example, the light will be lower while the temperature remains high. If you're using a heater, you're also decreasing the relative humidity in your space—which can lead to those crispy leaf tips. (More on humidity on page 14). Fortunately, average room temperatures between 65°F and 75°F will suit most houseplants.

The profiles in this book note who likes it hot and who might get cold feet. Remember that sudden changes in temperature, like turning on heating in cooler months, can stress out certain plants. Do you get concerned when the vibe shifts dramatically with someone you've been dating? It's the same with plants and temperature!

GETTING DRINKS

Just like you, plants need water to survive. That may seem pretty simple, but not all houseplants need the same amount or frequency of watering. Some are really thirsty, and others are more self-sufficient (like silver bracts on page 90, which have water-storing mechanisms). Figuring out your plant's ideal watering schedule will require you to spend some time learning what makes them thrive. It can be tricky at first, but it'll become second nature the more you get to know your potted partner.

The most common way to water your plants is "over the rim." This is when you pour water in the space between the top of the soil and the rim of the pot. All indoor gardeners should use a small watering can with a long spout, which allows you to direct the water into one place. You'll also want to make sure your planter has drainage holes. Always allow water to seep through the soil and drain through to a saucer. Letting your plants stay wet is actually *not* ideal since that's the quickest route to root rot—yuck. Tip out any excess water from the saucer when you're done. Moist is good; wet, soaked, and drowning is not.

Alternatively, some plants prefer bottom-watering. This technique is best for ones with hairy or soft leaves that can be damaged by moisture, like the velvety purple passion (page 50). Stand the pot in a bowl of shallow water, letting the roots and soil drink from the bottom up. This technique can take a longer time, but who doesn't like a quality slow jam every once in a while, right? When moisture rises to the surface of the soil, remove the pot and allow any excess water to drain.

Timing is everything when it comes to life and love, and this is especially true with watering. More plants die from too little or too much water than for any other reason. Just like when you're dating, you'll want to strike a balance between coming on too strong and completely ghosting them! When in doubt under water rather than over water. A plant can bounce back from lack of thirst—just don't tease them too much. Every plant has different needs, but there are a few practical ways you can judge when to water: Try pushing your finger about 2 inches into the soil. If it feels moist, don't water! You can also lift the pot to feel the weight—a lighter pot means the soil is dry.

GETTING STEAMY

Oh, the humidity! The amount of water in the air affects the health and growth of greenery. Some plants crave it, while others don't really care. Figure out which ones need it so you can set the mood for a great date—and great relationship.

Generally, tropical plants and plants with thin, fragile leaves love a humid atmosphere. Desert cacti and succulents with thick leaves, stems, and stalks don't need it. You can use a digital hygrometer to determine the humidity level in your space, but you probably don't have to get too high-tech. The simplest thing is to consider the climate you live in. Are you in a desert region where the air stays mostly dry? Or are you sweating it out in a subtropical paradise? You'll also want to think about how the conditions change with the seasons. Do heating and air-conditioning dry out your home?

If you've fallen for a plant that needs extra moisture, there are things you can do to create humidity. Getting plants together and standing them in small groups automatically creates a humid microclimate. You can also create a pebble tray by filling a saucer with some small stones, adding water (make sure the water doesn't rise above the pebbles), then setting your pot on top of the pebbles. As the water evaporates, it will bless the leaves with moist air. Humidifiers and misters can also help. Before you spritz your plant with a mister, though, be sure to check your plant's individual misting requirements (if they have any)—it could be pointless for some, and potentially lead to diseases in more sensitive types.

GETTING DIRTY

The dating world is full of mixed signals, and this extends to the plant world, too. When we talk about "soil" we're really referring to potting mix (also called "potting medium," "potting compost," or "soil-free mix"). Indoor plants need more than garden soil, which is too dense and variable, so they grow in a special premade blend of ingredients. Standard potting mix, or all-purpose potting mix, is your best bet for most houseplants. It tends to have more coarse mediums (perlite, charcoal, bark), which provide better aeration than outdoor mixes. It's light and airy, allows for easy drainage, and provides nutrients. If you can, choose an organic option and skip moisture-control mixes.

In addition to potting mix, you might need some extras to help avoid common issues and cater to specific plants. Perlite is a white volcanic glass compound that you can stir into potting mix. It helps roots grow and prevents them from suffocating by creating spaces within soil. Adding sand or vermiculite can also improve aeration and drainage. Cactus and succulent mix (which can also be used for palms) is quick-draining because these plants don't like soggy roots. Orchid bark, which is made primarily of tree bark, is good for bromeliads (page 101) and houseplants with larger root systems, like monsteras (page 37). There's some more advanced methods out there, such as semi-hydro with the use of leca (clay pebbles), but for the sake of successfully getting to first base, we'll stay focused on plants that thrive with coarse potting mix in this book.

How to
Meet the One

Now that you've evaluated your space and covered the basics of plant care, it's time to hit the scene. Just like the modern dating world, there are so many ways to find a plant that's right for you.

HOT SINGLES IN YOUR AREA

The rising popularity of houseplants has made them more widely available than ever. They're even merchandised as impulse purchases at supermarkets and big-box stores. Ideally, however, you want to go to a dedicated plant shop, garden center, or nursery. The people who work there are experts who know all about the plants they're selling. They can answer any questions you have and offer advice based on your space, needs, and lifestyle. Pour your heart out to them—they're there to help you on your journey to find love!

If you have "a type" (that is, you're looking for a specific plant), bring a picture to the plant shop and ask if they have it available. If not, they can often do a custom order with their vendors. Are you open to exploring something new? You might be into variegated species. Variegation is the appearance of different colors or markings on one plant due to lack of chlorophyll, which leads to fun contrasting spots, stripes, borders, and other designs. Some plants with the most eye-catching variegations include pothos, snake plants, monsteras, and philodendrons.

Take your time going through the plant shop and checking out what they have. Look for red flags while you browse. Avoid droopy, dried, or crispy plants with yellowing or browned leaves—they're not healthy and will leave you brokenhearted. Touch the leaves of succulents to check that they're firm, not wrinkly. Peek under leaves to make sure your potential partner doesn't have any skeletons in their closet—for plants, this might include leaf bugs or infested soil.

Ready to bring your plant home? When you finish a date, it's a courtesy to offer a ride or otherwise ensure your partner gets home safely. Similarly, you should think about how you'll transport your plant. Not only will it make a good impression, but it will be a healthy start to your relationship. Use a cardboard box that ensures the plant won't tip over on the trip. You can even wrap the plant in plastic sheeting or paper for extra protection.

ONLINE DATING

Going online has made it more accessible to find a connection, whether it's with people or plants! This is especially helpful if you don't have great plant shops in your area or if you don't have the means to safely transport a plant back to yours. Online plant sellers are also a helpful source if you're seeking something that you haven't been able to find IRL. Before you hit the Buy button, check any reviews and ratings. You should also manage your expectations by being aware of seasonal and regional shipping restrictions. Think about the costs, too. You'll likely find a huge range of price points for the plant you want, but shipping can be expensive. Properly packing a plant to ensure it doesn't get damaged in transit comes with a fee.

It's common to experience a premature evacuation when unboxing your plant—soil typically comes loose in transit and can make a mess when you open the package. (Hey, it happens to the best of us!) So when unboxing your plant, do it outside, if possible. You can also lay down newspaper on a flat, steady surface, then place the package on top before opening.

The houseplant community has a great online presence, too. Check out the social apps for a plant group in your area to find other enthusiasts or even to make trades for cuttings. Lots of local plant shops will also host events like plant swaps, so get involved in your local houseplant community!

Keeping the Love Alive

You're past the dating stage, and you've made it official! Relationships inevitably change when you move in together, and the same goes with greenery. Here are some brief pointers for cohabitation with chlorophyll companions.

PHYSICAL ATTRACTION

It's easy to let go of ourselves in long-term relationships. It's all part of getting more comfortable, but things can get rough when we neglect to care for ourselves and each other. With plants, grooming is an essential part of care. It also keeps them looking their best! Indoor plants accumulate dust and dirt on their leaves, which clog their pores and prevent growth. Give them some spa time by gently wiping down leaves with a damp cloth. For plants that don't like to get their leaves wet,

you can use a soft, clean paintbrush. Tweezers or a brush will work for any debris stuck in a hairy cactus.

You can make a plant fuller and more symmetrical by tidying stems and shoots. It also stimulates growth. Think of it like a haircut! You can use sharp scissors or pruning shears on a stem or stalk to clip back the shape—cut it just above a leaf joint. Remove dead and yellow leaves by simply pinching them off between a finger and thumb.

OFFERING SUPPORT

Don't you want a supportive partner? So do plants! There are certain species that benefit from extra support to keep them upright. Moss poles, green Velcro plant tape, string or twine, plastic frameworks, and metal rings for those long runners (or leafless growths) are common accessories. First, tie the string to the support, then loop it around the plant stem just below a leaf joint. You might have to tie it in a few places depending on the plant's size and shape. Climbing plants like vines can often be wound around special hoops and poles.

NURTURING THE RELATIONSHIP

Some people say that food is the language of love. Plants would probably agree with those people. Many potting mixes contain fertilizers that will give plants the nutrients they need for about six months; thereafter, it's likely your houseplant will need some plant food every now and then. This will keep it healthy and growing strong. There are different types of fertilizer from slow-release pellets to liquid you can add to water, so research what's on the market and what's most compatible with your plant. In general, plants should be fed during spring and summer, which is their active growth period.

MOVING ON

There comes a point when you might outgrow certain aspects of a relationship. When a plant ages, their roots can outgrow their container, or they might need a soil refresh after their potting mix becomes compacted. "Up-potting" is when you move your plant to a larger container if you want to give it more space to continue growing, versus "repotting," which is when you move a plant to a container of the same size to check on its roots or add some slow-release fertilizer. You should up-pot when you see exposed roots on top of the pot or coming out through drainage holes.

The process for repotting or up-potting is fairly simple. Gently pull your plant out of its current pot, then use your hands to comb through the roots to loosen the soil. Pour some fresh potting mix into the new container and place the plant inside the pot. Try to aim for an inch between the top of the soil line and the top of the pot. You can remove the plant and add more soil to the bottom of the pot if it's coming up short. Once it looks good, fill the edges around the plant with more potting mix (and add your fertilizer, if desired!).

Relationship Problems

No relationship is perfect. There's bound to be some issues and growing pains. When there's trouble in paradise, try to identify the problem and work on it. (With plants, act as quickly as possible!) You should always research your specific plant, but here are some common issues you might face as a couple.

DRY OR DEAD LEAVES

Leaves might drop for several reasons, including a sudden change in temperature, humidity, or light. If this is the case, reposition your plant in a spot with warm, even temperatures away from drafts or dry air from a heater. Yellowing leaves that eventually drop off are a result of overwatering or a deficient diet. Scale back on the watering or try some plant food. When leaves appear crisp and turn brown, it's likely they need more water and/or humidty.

ROOT ROT

This common problem is caused by excessive watering, insufficient drainage, or putting a plant in a pot that's too big or small. Too much moisture in the soil can allow fungus to grow in the soil and attack the roots. If you've identified root rot, remove the plant from its pot and remove all the soil. Cut off any roots that are black,

brown, or soft. Disinfect your pots to prevent the fungus from spreading, then repot your plant in fresh potting mix and hope for the best.

LEGGINESS

A plant is "leggy" or creates "runners" when the stems grow long and thin, stretching out or leaning to one side with just a few leaves on top. This happens when the plant isn't getting enough light or is only getting light from a single direction. It becomes heliotropic, or starts desperately reaching out toward the light. Consider moving your plant to a spot that receives more direct light, regularly rotating your plant, or investing in a grow light. Leggy stems can't be restored to thick, luscious growth, so you may want to snip them off (and grow the cuttings for a friend or swap). If you do, make the cut just above a leaf joint or node.

PESTS

The best method for pest control is prevention. Healthy plants are less likely to be attacked by bugs, so try to keep on top of your plant care. Some of the most common pests you may encounter include fungus gnats (they resemble fruit flies), spider mites (they build fine webs), aphids and scale insects (they create a sticky residue), and mealybugs (they look like little fluffs of white cotton). If you spot these culprits early enough, they can often be exterminated with simple first aid, like physically removing them with a cotton swab, repotting a plant, or wiping down leaves with soapy water. My favorite preemptive process is mixing 1 part alcohol, 1 part peroxide, and 2 parts water into a spray bottle and spraying the leaves (make sure to get the undersides, too!) once a month or so, especially during the warmer months when pests tend to emerge or be most prevalent. If the infestation is extensive, you may need to get rid of the plant. Breakups happen all the time, so remember it's not the end of the world!

SICKNESS AND DISEASE

Just like dealing with pests, good plant care is the best way to prevent disease. Root rot is one of the more likely "sicknesses" you'll detect (see page 23), but there's also mold and powdery mildew—*yuck!* When you see this on leaves, completely remove any affected parts of the plant and try to improve the conditions that may have led to the infection. It'll help to do some research on your plant and its specific environment, but infection could be due to overwatering, lack of air circulation, or too much fertilizer.

A Mutually Beneficial Relationship

We talk a lot about "healthy relationships" in dating, and hook-ups are great, especially when the lead to something long-lasting and make our lives better. Houseplants have positive effects on our literal health, both psychologically and physically. Their presence can elevate mood, reduce stress and fatigue, and even lower blood pressure and heart rate. The reasons behind this are still being studied, but the simple activity of plant care is undoubtedly an act of self-care, too. Caring for a plant promotes a positive outlook on life, such that psychologists have developed "horticultural therapy" programs to help people deal with loneliness, anxiety, and depression. In an age where we spend more time indoors, disconnected from people and nature, and when homes are increasingly becoming places of work, this is especially important. Trust me—I was an anxious and then depressed Californian living on the East Coast. Then I got a bunch of plants and started living my best life. Plants can change your life if you let them.

There's even more stuff that we also love to see: Studies have shown that many houseplants improve air quality. Research by NASA revealed that some plants reduce volatile organic pollutants such as benzene, formaldehyde, and tricho-loethane. These substances can be present in indoor air and are linked to a variety of health problems. The actual impact in home environments is debatable, but plants that are credited with air-purifying qualities include aloe vera (page 77) and the ZZ plant (page 98).

Spread the Love

Sharing is caring! Trading plants and sharing cuttings is a fun, rewarding way to build friendships or give gifts. "Propagation" is when you create a new plant from an existing one, and it's simpler than you might think. There are different propagation methods that suit different plants, but the most common technique is taking a leaf cutting or stem cutting and putting it in water, where roots will grow. (This won't work for all plants, but you can try it with pothos (page 46 and 62), philodendron (page 73 and 94), and hoya (page 69 and 74), among others.) Make sure you create a cutting with nodes or growth points for future stems!

To take a cutting, use clean shears or a pair of scissors and cut a piece of stem just below a node. The node is a bump or spot that leaves grow out of. Your cutting should be at least five inches long. Pop the cutting into a vessel of water—like a mason jar, bud vase, or whatever reusable clear container you have that fits the bill—and new roots will sprout in the coming weeks. Don't forget to change the water, too!

When the roots are a few inches long, you can repot your propagated plant or give the cutting to someone, even if they're far away. If you're shipping a cutting, wrap the roots in a wet paper towel. Then, enclose the towel-wrapped roots in a small plastic bag. Use a twist tie to secure the top of the bag, making sure all leaves pop out at the top. (They should be exposed, not sealed in the plastic.) Package the cutting in a box that is filled with newspaper and send it away using the fastest shipping option available.

Propagating is also a sustainable, eco-friendly way to increase your own plant collection—and it lets you do so without spending any money. Talk about a cheap date! You can find local or online plant communities with people who are willing to offer advice and even cuttings. This can be a great way to get rare cuttings of plants that aren't widely available where you live. Don't be afraid to reach out and connect. Stop doomscrolling and instead take a shelfie of your plant collection, post a hashtag, and get engaged! Tag #houseplanthookups #thedirtonplants and follow @agathatisabel to stay connected and be part of our community!

Get ready to meet eligible epiphytes, playful philodendrons, hoya hook-ups, and more!

The plant profiles in the next section are tongue-in-cheek, but all the information is based in fact. You'll find real tips that teach you how to look after 35 possible plant partners. And if you're still not sure what you want in a plant partner, check out the Plant-Based Personality Quiz on page 102 or the Quick & Dirty Index on page 108, which shows plants by difficulty level, pet-friendliness, and more.

Each plant profile has the following information to help you find your match.

Originally from: Houseplants have a rich history and come from all over the world. This lets you see where a plant originally rooted from. #HOESINDIFFERENTAREACODES.

Light: Does a plant need bright light or is it happy to hang in the shade? This is the recommended light intensity for the plant, including specifics about whether the light should be indirect, direct, diffuse, and more.

BRIGHT: Your space gets about 5 to 8 hours of direct light.

AVERAGE: Your space gets sun for part of the day.

LOW: Your space doesn't get any direct sunlight, and it's mainly shady. Many rooms become low-light spaces in the winter months when the sun sets earlier.

DIRECT OR INDIRECT: Some plants love direct sun, while others will scorch or prefer light that is filtered through curtains or blinds.

Water: Some houseplants love hydration, and others don't. These ratings give a general idea of how often you'll need to tend to them (Low, Regular, High). For the purposes of this book, Regular watering means once a week, but you can turn to page 13 for more details.

Humidity: Humidity is another source of water for plants, and some need more than others.

> **LOW:** Below 50 percent
>
> **NORMAL:** 50 to 60 percent
>
> **HIGH:** 60 to 80 percent

Temperature: The temperature of most homes ranges from 65°F to 75°F. Here, this is what we consider to be Average temperature. Low is below 65°F, and High is above 75°F.

Difficulty: This general rating from 1 to 3 tells you if a plant is low-maintenance or if it needs a lot of care and attention.

Now, use your green thumb to start swiping!

Alocasia Polly
ALOCASIA × AMAZONICA 'POLLY'

LIGHT: AVERAGE TO BRIGHT + INDIRECT
WATER: REGULAR + WELL-DRAINED
HUMIDITY: HIGH
TEMPERATURE: AVERAGE TO HIGH
DIFFICULTY: 2

ORIGINALLY FROM SOUTHEAST ASIA. If you're new to plant-based dating, you might want to swipe to the next profile. I need someone who knows their way around some potting soil to get my ruffled leaves to flourish.

You'll have to get used to
My mood swings. One day I'll be feeling my best, leaves ready to take on the world . . . and then BAM! It's droop city. Like everyone, I have my ups and downs, but it's totally normal. Just check that my soil isn't too dry (I like it to be kept moist), and make sure I'm getting a good amount of indirect light, and I should get back on track.

Something I'll never do again
Sunbathe. If you have fair skin, you might feel my pain. I love sunshine, but direct light will scorch or bleach my glossy, silver-veined dark-green leaves.

My motto is
The more the merrier! If you have other plants at home, I'm willing to explore an open relationship. You see, I thrive in humidity, so it helps to keep me close to other plants. If you'd like us to be exclusive, then make sure you mist me daily.

Don't hate me if
I ghost you during cuffing season. It's not you—it's me. Really! I go dormant in the winter months. Just put me in a warm spot, reduce my watering, and by the time spring rolls around I'll be good to go.

Snake Plant

SANSEVIERIA TRIFASCIATA

LIGHT: LOW TO BRIGHT + INDIRECT
WATER: LOW
HUMIDITY: NORMAL
TEMPERATURE: AVERAGE TO HIGH
DIFFICULTY: 1

ORIGINALLY FROM WEST AFRICA. Maybe you've also heard me called Mother-In-Law's Tongue, and no offense to your partner's mom, but I'm much easier to get along with than that name suggests. I'm perfect for beginners because I'm super easy to maintain and difficult to kill. You can put me anywhere: the floor, on a desk, or anyplace that needs some sharp style.

I'm not afraid to

Give second chances. Or third chances. I'm known for being very forgiving. You can ghost me for weeks at a time, and my leaves will still look sharp, bright, and fresh. Who has time for grudges? Forgiving and forgetting is so much cooler. I'm easygoing like that.

My best feature is

Snakeskin is always in season! Regardless of the variegation, my hardy patterned leaves are the perfect accessory for any room.

This year, I really want to

Try out Dry January . . . and February. It's not the most imaginative New Year's resolution, but in winter I can go for up to 2 months without water. Overwatering can actually give me root rot, so I'd love to cut back on the beverages until spring.

Monstera Deliciosa

MONSTERA DELICIOSA

LIGHT: AVERAGE TO BRIGHT + INDIRECT
WATER: REGULAR
HUMIDITY: NORMAL TO HIGH
TEMPERATURE: AVERAGE TO HIGH
DIFFICULTY: 2

ORIGINALLY FROM CENTRAL AMERICA. You've likely already seen me all over the internet—from bedrooms to wedding decor, people look toward my distinct leaves to add tropical flair to whatever room I'm in. At this point, I might even seem a bit passé, but my striking looks and minimal care regimen make me a big deal in the houseplant world.

I have a reputation for

Getting around. I'm originally from Central America, but I've been known to pop up all over the globe. From the Hawaiian Islands to Lake Como, Italy, and the Mediterranean, to Singapore and the Philippines, I can thrive in tropical, subtropical, and even in temperate areas during their warmer months.

My best feature is

My fenestrations, a fancy name for holes, which have led to me affectionally being called the Swiss Cheese Plant. Plus, they're not only cool to look at, they're also extremely practical. The holes and ribbons allow me to withstand downpours or extreme weather, and the larger surface area means I can take advantage of the usually minimal light that makes it way down to the ground in my native tropical forests.

I'm not afraid to

Take up space. Like I said, I'm a big deal, and I do mean big. If you live in a studio apartment, I might not be the best match for you. I can grow about 1 to 2 feet in height a year, and my leaves can get up to 3 feet long.

Round-Leaf Calathea

CALATHEA ORBIFOLIA

LIGHT: LOW TO AVERAGE + INDIRECT
WATER: REGULAR
HUMIDITY: HIGH
TEMPERATURE: HIGH
DIFFICULTY: 3

ORIGINALLY FROM SOUTH AMERICA. If you've come across my profile, you must be serious enough about finding the right match to pay for the premium subscription. That's a good thing, too, because it's going to take a real commitment to make things work between us. I have very particular needs when it comes to water, light, temperature, and living conditions, so the more experienced the partner, the better.

I can be a bit

Fragile. My roots are thin and delicate, so choosing the right soil can be a make-or-break situation. An airy, lightweight potting mix with good water retention works best.

My zodiac sign is

I don't know my whole chart, but I'm definitely not a water sign. Watering errors are usually where things go wrong in my relationships. Getting the right balance can be tricky, but it's best to wait until the top few inches of soil are dry before watering again.

Green flags I look for

Greenhouse conditions. Think tropical! I thrive in moisture-laden air and warm temps. To keep me looking my best, set me somewhere with humidity levels of at least 50 percent. If your climate is on the drier side, a pebble tray, humidifier, or regular misting can help.

Rubber Tree

FICUS ELASTICA

LIGHT: BRIGHT + INDIRECT

WATER: HIGH

HUMIDITY: NORMAL

TEMPERATURE: AVERAGE TO HIGH

DIFFICULTY: 2

ORIGINALLY FROM SOUTHEAST ASIA. I'm irresistible: I'm tall, dark (green), and handsome. Despite what my name suggests, I don't bounce back like rubber, so you might want to get some plant-partner experience before bringing me home. Once we settle into a routine, though, I can grow to be up to 10 feet tall.

My biggest fear
Like many people (and plants!), I'm scared of change. If you want to move me to a different spot, we'll have to take things slowly and do it gradually. Even the slightest shift in my conditions and care will cause my waxy leaves to suddenly drop.

My biggest failure
I always end up exposing myself. That's because I can outgrow my soil, which leaves my roots exposed. When this happens, simply top me up with some more.

I'm looking for someone who
Can give me support. I tend to droop as I grow and get heavier, so I'll need a long wooden dowel or bamboo stalk to keep me standing upright.

Spider Plant
CHLOROPHYTUM COMOSUM

LIGHT: LOW TO BRIGHT + INDIRECT
WATER: REGULAR
HUMIDITY: NORMAL TO HIGH
TEMPERATURE: AVERAGE TO HIGH
DIFFICULTY: 1

ORIGINALLY FROM CENTRAL AND SOUTHERN AFRICA. Listen, I get why it stuck, but looks-wise, I couldn't be further from my creepy-crawly 8-legged namesake. Thankfully, people seem to see past the nickname, and I'm actually one of the most popular houseplants out there—probably because I'm easy to grow and I'm a fun hang. My long, ribbonlike leaves grow over 12 inches long, so they're perfect for a hanging planter.

The key to my heart is
Being a good tipper. If the tips of my leaves turn brown, it's likely that the air around me is too dry (in which case, mist me regularly) or I might be getting too much direct sunlight (in which case, put me in a shadier spot).

Don't be surprised if I
Fall head over heels. In addition to my long leaves, I regularly sprout stems with adorable baby plantlets, which can get heavy. Not only are you a person I could fall for, but I can also literally fall off a shelf or table if I'm not properly supported.

My secret talent
I'm an air purifier! I have the special ability to clean indoor air by removing pollutants. If you invite a few of my friends over and keep a bunch of us together in a small space, you might notice a difference.

Bird of Paradise
STRELITZIA NICOLAI

LIGHT: LOW TO BRIGHT
WATER: HIGH
HUMIDITY: HIGH
TEMPERATURE: AVERAGE TO HIGH
DIFFICULTY: 3

ORIGINALLY FROM SOUTH AFRICA. I'm like a supermodel—I can reach over 6 feet tall, and I'm breathtakingly beautiful, with great stems. I don't even have a trunk—your tender, loving care can be the only support I need. I'm pretty hardy for a tropical plant and can adapt well to indoor living, but if you keep me in a pot that can be moved outside in summer, I will truly thrive, not just survive.

Don't be concerned if
I want to take a break. It's natural for my large, tropical leaves to break apart, and it happens all the time when I'm grown in the wild. Just because I'm prone to splitting, doesn't mean we should split up.

My must-have accessory
A pebble tray or humidifier. Love is in the air when there's moisture in the air! I like my soil to remain moist—though never wet or soggy—and appreciate humid environments.

I have a reputation for
Bugging out. When grown indoors, I have a tendency to attract mealybugs. If left untreated, these pests can kill me, but thankfully, all you need to do is remove any white powder with rubbing alcohol. To prevent infestations, mix rubbing alcohol and dish soap in a spray bottle and give me a good misting.

Golden Pothos

EPIPREMNUM PINNATUM CV. 'AUREUM'

LIGHT: LOW TO BRIGHT + INDIRECT
WATER: REGULAR
HUMIDITY: NORMAL TO HIGH
TEMPERATURE: AVERAGE
DIFFICULTY: 1

ORIGINALLY FROM SOUTHEAST ASIA AND THE PACIFIC ISLANDS. I've got a lot of ambition, and I'm always searching for what's next, climbing over anything that gets in my way! But I'm not cutthroat about it. Usually I'm pretty chill, content to just hang around and go with the flow.

We'll get along if
You're down with personal growth. I'm all about self-empowerment, and with little help, I can add over a foot of growth in a single month.

My most irrational fear
Identity theft. While a philodendron (page 94) might look similar, the difference is in our leaves. My textured, heart-shaped leaves are large and thick and waxy. Philodendron leaves are more distinctively heart-shaped and are thinner, softer, and smoother.

My nickname is
Among other things, I've been called Devil's Ivy, but I don't think it's an insult. It just means that I'm super hard to kill.

Boobie Cactus

**MYRTILLOCACTUS GEOMETRIZANS
'FUKUROKURYUZINBOKU'**

LIGHT: BRIGHT + INDIRECT
WATER: LOW
HUMIDITY: LOW
TEMPERATURE: HIGH
DIFFICULTY: 1

ORIGINALLY FROM CENTRAL AND NORTHERN MEXICO. Despite my potentially NSFW name, my low-maintenance succulent needs mean that I'm actually a great cubicle mate. My blue-green bumps and sometimes-flowering spikes will make me the talk of your weekly 1:1.

My karaoke song is
"My Humps" by the Black Eyed Peas

We'll get along if
You're willing to take things slow. I can take time to reach my full potential, but I promise I'm worth the wait. To speed things along, you can water and fertilize me in the summer months, but when winter comes, I prefer to keep things close to my warm-climate origins and stay dry since too much water will make me rot—yuck!

I have a reputation for
Playing hard to get. While my parent family (Myrtillocactus geometrizans) can happily thrive outside, I don't naturally occur and was specifically cultivated in Japanese nurseries to be an indoor plant. I can only be grown through propagating a clipping, so you might have to stop by a few plant stores to find me.

Purple Passion

GYNURA AURANTIACA

LIGHT: AVERAGE TO BRIGHT + INDIRECT

WATER: REGULAR

HUMIDITY: NORMAL

TEMPERATURE: AVERAGE

DIFFICULTY: 2

ORIGINALLY FROM INDONESIA. Is there anything more seductive and luxurious than purple velvet? Call me biased, but I don't think so. My dark green leaves are coated in a soft violet fuzz. And I'm here to bring passion into your bedroom . . . or any room where I can receive filtered, indirect sunlight.

I love anyone who uses

A shower cap. I need regular watering and moist soil to stay healthy, but I get waterlogged if liquid gets trapped in my hairs. Try to avoid spilling water on my leaves!

Something you can't tell by my photos

My receding hairline. Just like many humans, my hair thins out as I get older. When this happens, I might lose some of my brightness, too. If that sounds unappealing, just remember that all beauty fades, but love is forever!

My biggest failure is

My BO. Hey, we can't all smell like roses! When I reach maturity, I can grow orange flowers under certain conditions. These blooms have a pretty bad stink, but you can just remove them to get rid of the unwelcome aroma.

My favorite musician

Prince. How can I resist *Purple Rain*? It's my favorite album. And song. And movie.

Watermelon Peperomia

PILEA ARGYREIA

LIGHT: LOW TO BRIGHT + INDIRECT
WATER: REGULAR + WELL-DRAINED
HUMIDITY: NORMAL TO HIGH
TEMPERATURE: AVERAGE TO HIGH
DIFFICULTY: 2

ORIGINALLY FROM SOUTH AFRICA. Not to get too ahead of ourselves, but let's admit that moving in with a partner can be challenging, especially if they're bringing all of their things with them. Well, that won't be an issue with me! I'm a compact little cutie who doesn't need a lot of room. What I lack in size, I make up for in good looks. My vibrant patterned leaves, which resemble watermelon rinds, and bright red stems are a total aesthetic.

Something you can't tell from my photos

It's hard to miss my striking leaves, but the camera doesn't pick up the way they shimmer, especially when the sunlight hits me! You'll have to get off the app and meet me IRL to really see me shine.

Don't hate me if

The conversation runs dry. It doesn't mean I'm uninterested! I just like to make sure my soil dries out between waterings. I'm not happy when I'm overwatered, so don't let me be too damp for too long.

I want someone who

Can turn up the heat! I'm a "radiator plant," which means I love warm air. But if you don't want to sweat it out, that's okay, too—I'm willing to live with normal household temperatures. Compromise is part of any healthy relationship, right?

Fiddle-Leaf Fig

FICUS LYRATA

LIGHT: BRIGHT + INDIRECT
WATER: REGULAR + WELL-DRAINED
HUMIDITY: NORMAL TO HIGH
TEMPERATURE: NORMAL
DIFFICULTY: 3

ORIGINALLY FROM WEST AFRICA. If you're up for a challenge, slide into my DMs (Dirt Messages!). I'll admit, I can be a bit of a handful, but I know what I like. I'm a tall showstopper, with a flair for the dramatic. But who wants a boring relationship, anyway?

Three words that describe me

Big, beautiful, and bossy. You could even call me a *fickle*-leaf fig: I need just the right amount of light, just the right amount of water, and just the right temperature. My violin-shaped leaves will be playing a sad tune if you don't treat me *juuuust* right.

A trend I can't get behind

Netflix and chill. I cannot stand the cold, and I will betray you if expose me to lower temps. Do *not* put me near an open vent, air conditioner, or anywhere drafty—you've been warned.

This year, I really want

What all the girlies want: a dewy glow and a detox. And I'll need your help with both. Mist me daily (especially if your home is low humidity), wipe me down weekly, and, once a month, flush my soil until the water runs out of the bottom of the pot.

Jade Plant
CRASSULA OVATA

LIGHT: BRIGHT + INDIRECT
WATER: REGULAR + WELL-DRAINED
HUMIDITY: LOW TO NORMAL
TEMPERATURE: AVERAGE
DIFFICULTY: 1

ORIGINALLY FROM SOUTH AFRICA. It's easy to get jaded when you're swiping through profiles. But I promise you won't get jaded with a jade plant. I'm an easygoing (and easy*growing*) companion. With minimal effort, I can live for a long time, so if you're more interested in a long-term commitment than a fling or a one-night stand, get in touch.

Don't be jealous if
I go home with other people. I'm extremely simple to propagate so you can spread the love around and still keep some for yourself.

I need a partner who
Can read my body language. As a succulent, I need a *lot* of sun—at least 4 hours of bright, indirect light a day, but if you don't hydrate me correctly, my leaves will let you know. If I'm puffy and swollen, I'm overwatered. If I start to shrivel, I'm parched. In the spring and summer, watering once a week should be good. I need even less in the colder months.

I have a reputation for
Being lucky. I'm said to bring good fortune and prosperity, especially when placed near your front door. Just don't place me in the bathroom—the principles of feng shui say that's as good as flushing money down the drain!

Anthurium Clarinervium

ANTHURIUM CLARINERVIUM

LIGHT: BRIGHT + INDIRECT
WATER: HIGH + WELL-DRAINED
HUMIDITY: HIGH
TEMPERATURE: AVERAGE TO HIGH
DIFFICULTY: 3

ORIGINALLY FROM MEXICO. My name kinda looks like the Latin motto for an Ivy League school, and as a rare type of the *Anthurium* genus, I'm just as elite as one of those universities. If you're lucky enough to come across me and treat me well, I'll give you my heart-shaped leaves!

I'm looking for someone who

Appreciates the beauty of an older partner. My contrasting white veins become more auspicious and eye-catching as I mature. So how about we make some long-term plans?

My nickname is

Velvet Cardboard Anthurium, named after the velvety, stiff texture of my leaves. Sure, it's easier to say if you're struggling with the Latin, but I think a houseplant of my pedigree should be called something a little more regal.

Biggest turn-off

Don't play hard to get. I'm fussy and high maintenance. To truly thrive, I need lots of light, lots of humidity, and lots of water (but not too much!), so you've got to let me know from the start you can take care of me the way I deserve.

Poinsettia
EUPHORBIA PULCHERRIMA

LIGHT: BRIGHT + INDIRECT
WATER: REGULAR + WELL-DRAINED
HUMIDITY: NORMAL TO HIGH
TEMPERATURE: AVERAGE
DIFFICULTY: 2

ORIGINALLY FROM MEXICO. You might be surprised to find me on here, but I'm tired of meeting someone during cuffing season, only to get dumped after the holidays. Sure, my red flowers and stems coupled with my green leaves get me a lot of action around Christmas, but then I'm on the curb with all the dead evergreens after I bloom. Can we normalize poinsettias as year-round houseplants? I'm ready for a long-term relationship.

This year, I really want to
Live to see another winter holiday! All you need to do is give me some warmth, some indirect sunlight, and a thorough watering whenever my soil gets dry. If you put me on a specific growing schedule (look it up!), you can even make me bloom again the next time the holidays roll around. How's that for sustainability?

My nickname is
My fiery blooms have earned me the nickname Mexican Flameleaf. But don't worry, I'm actually a pretty chill plant. I've got red flowers, not red flags!

Something you can't tell by my photos
I like things steamy. Putting my pot on a pebble tray filled with stones and water is a great humidity hack to keep me happy in dry homes.

Cebu Blue

EPIPREMNUM PINNATUM 'CEBU BLUE'

LIGHT: LOW TO BRIGHT + INDIRECT
WATER: REGULAR
HUMIDITY: LOW TO NORMAL
TEMPERATURE: AVERAGE
DIFFICULTY: 1

ORIGINALLY FROM THE PHILIPPINES. Despite my water, humidity, and temperature needs, I'd like to think I'm anything but average. If you look closely, and in the right light, my blue-green leaves have a shimmery silver glow. And unlike other members of the of the *Epipremnum* family, my leaves are long and thin, not heart shaped, making me as unique as I am easy to care for.

The award I should be nominated for

Yes, the Sampaguita is the national flower of the Philippines, but I think they should really consider adding a national plant. I'm originally from the islands' Cebu region, which is where I get my name.

My zodiac sign is

I'm an Aries, determined and restless. If left to my own devices in a hanging basket, I'll behave like your typical pothos and stretch as far as you'll let me. But give me pole, and I'll climb to my tendrils' content.

My secret talent

Shapeshifting. If you're in it for the long haul and allow me to reach maturation or happen to purchase a Cebu that's in its twenties, my signature leaves will begin to lose their blue hue and develop fenestrations. I'll look like a mini monstera! To aid this process along, you can mimic an environment closest to my home country and give me a moss pole to climb so I feel like I'm in the rainforest.

Sensitive Plant

MIMOSA PUDICA

LIGHT: BRIGHT + DIRECT
WATER: REGULAR + WELL-DRAINED
HUMIDITY: HIGH
TEMPERATURE: NORMAL
DIFFICULTY: 2

ORIGINALLY FROM CENTRAL AND SOUTH AMERICA. Are you looking for a sensitive partner? Although I'm the sensitive type, I'm no wallflower or shrinking violet. My sensitivity comes from tiny hairs that respond to stimulus. If you touch me, my leaves immediately fold up. Hey, that tickles!

My nickname is
Sometimes people call me Touch-Me-Not, but it's by no means a direct order. Although I might recoil if you touch me, I won't hurt you. You won't hurt me, either, so long as you treat me right: I need lots of light and my soil should be allowed to completely dry out before watering me again.

My love language is
Physical touch. *Duh.* It's so stimulating!

You should not message me if
You're a night owl. If you like to stay up late, we probably won't be a good match. My leaves don't just close when I'm prodded—they also shut at night.

My secret talent
I'm a cheerleader! Don't believe me? Just watch me bloom. I can grow short-lived purple flowers in the summer that look like pom-poms. I'm also known for being leggy, which is perfect for those high kicks. (You can prevent me from getting too leggy with regular pruning to keep my appearance full and bushy.)

String of Pearls

CURIO ROWLEYANUS

LIGHT: BRIGHT + INDIRECT
WATER: LOW + WELL-DRAINED
HUMIDITY: LOW
TEMPERATURE: LOW TO HIGH
DIFFICULTY: 2

ORIGINALLY FROM SOUTHWEST AFRICA. Yes, my long, trailing stems with their spherical leaves are as elegant as an expensive pearl necklace, but I'm not as high maintenance as my name might suggest. If you pay some attention to my light intake and watering schedule, I'll be an easygoing plant partner who would never string you along.

My favorite time of day is

I'm a morning person. I love chilling in the soft morning light! When the harsh afternoon sun rolls around, move me to a spot that with more shade.

If I were a drink I'd be

A glass of Sauv Blanc. I like things on the drier side, and I'm very sensitive to overwatering, so only water me once every couple of weeks and keep me out of rooms with high humidity like bathrooms and kitchens.

My most irrational fear

Wet feet! Ew, gross! Please make sure my soil is well-draining and my pot has sufficient holes, otherwise I'm susceptible to root rot.

Sweetheart Plant

HOYA KERRI

LIGHT: BRIGHT + INDIRECT
WATER: LOW
HUMIDITY: NORMAL TO HIGH
TEMPERATURE: AVERAGE TO HIGH
DIFFICULTY: 1

ORIGINALLY FROM SOUTHEAST ASIA. One look at my adorable, waxy heart-shaped leaves, and I'm sure you'll be all heart-eyes emoji. I'm not asking for much, just a sunny windowsill and some water every once in a while. What can I say? I'm a lover, not a fighter.

This year, I really want to

Let my roots down. Sure, one single heart-shaped leaf is incredibly cute, but unfortunately, if that's how you buy me, that's all I'll ever be! For a longer-term relationship with true growth potential, opt for a full plant so I can sprout new branches and leaves.

You might be surprised to learn

I can produce white and red flowers that smell like sugar or caramel. I'm a slow grower, and won't bloom until I'm 2 to 4 years old, but if you make sure I get sunlight every day and don't overwater me, you'll eventually be rewarded.

We'll get along if

You like alone time. Leave me to my own devices, unwatered and unbothered, in a sunny spot for weeks, and the next time you check up on me I may have a new leaf or peduncle or both. My peduncles, or spurs, are where my flowers bloom from, so leave those alone, too!

Fishbone Cactus

DISOCACTUS ANGULIGER

LIGHT: BRIGHT + INDIRECT
WATER: REGULAR
HUMIDITY: NORMAL TO HIGH
TEMPERATURE: AVERAGE TO HIGH
DIFFICULTY: 2

ORIGINALLY FROM MEXICO. I know, I know—indoor cacti have a bad rap. We need to soak up a lot of light, we're easy to overwater, and we've been known to drop off out of the blue. But don't swipe to the next profile. I swear I'm not like the others! I don't need direct sunlight—all I need is your love.

I can be a bit

Picky (and prickly). So I know what I said . . . but I'm still a cactus and can use just a *little* bit of pampering. The thing is, the chemicals in hard water, don't agree with me, so I'd appreciate distilled water, if you can. And before you roll your eyes, just know that your doting will be rewarded with beautiful pink flowers once I reach maturity. (Just don't blink or you'll miss them. They only stick around for a day or two.)

My most irrational fear

Being in the spotlight. I'm happy to sit back so you can shine! Unlike desert cacti, I naturally grow from tree branches under a forest canopy. So I prefer indirect or dappled light and won't mind if your place doesn't get enough sun.

My ideal first date

I'm down to get high. A hanging planter is one of the best ways to display my unique zigzag leaves.

Pink Princess Philodendron

PHILODENDRON ERUBESCENS 'PINK PRINCESS'

LIGHT: LOW TO BRIGHT + INDIRECT
WATER: REGULAR + WELL-DRAINED
HUMIDITY: NORMAL TO HIGH
TEMPERATURE: AVERAGE TO HIGH
DIFFICULTY: 2

ORIGINS UNKNOWN. Looking for someone to treat like royalty? I'm one of the most coveted houseplants in the kingdom, admired near and far for my vibrant pink variegation. But a houseplant of my pedigree isn't easy to come by, and I have a high price tag befitting my title—I might set you back hundreds of dollars. However, if you have the means, my beauty is worth every pretty penny.

I want someone who
Will be a loyal subject. Although I can survive in low light with average humidity, I appreciate devotion and reward those who can give me the specific care I truly desire. If you want to see me with larger, more vivd leaves, I need bright, indirect light and a boost of humidity from occasional misting.

Never have I ever
Had a cosmetic procedure. No judgment if people want to get a little work done, but there's some wannabes out there that try to copy my natural beauty. Don't get *plant*fished by the Pink Congo philodendron: She might look like me, but chemicals injected into her leaves give a fake pink variegation that eventually fades back to green.

My favorite movies are
Pretty in Pink, Legally Blonde, and *The Princess Diaries.* Need I explain?

Hindu Rope Plant
HOYA CARNOSA 'COMPACTA'

LIGHT: LOW TO BRIGHT + INDIRECT
WATER: LOW
HUMIDITY: NORMAL
TEMPERATURE: AVERAGE TO HIGH
DIFFICULTY: 1

ORIGINALLY FROM EAST ASIA AND AUSTRALIA. If you're a plant novice, I'll show you the ropes. Although I can be a slow grower, there's no need to wait for us to get to know each other better—I'm actually showing you *my* ropes right now. If you're looking for a plant pal that's as easy to keep alive as it is fun to look at, it's time to stop swiping and say hiya to this hoya.

Something you can't tell by my photos
You might take one look at my ribbon-like foliage and think I need special care, but my twisted curls are surprisingly low maintenance. I can tolerate most lighting conditions (though brighter light helps my foliage become more vibrant), and I don't need to be watered often.

My motto is
Absence makes the heart grow fonder. It's best to leave me alone and refrain from watering until my soil is completely dry. As a semi-succulent, my thick leaves already store a lot of water. If I start getting droopy, I'm probably overwatered and could do with a break.

A deal breaker
Horror fans. I don't like scary movies and cannot deal with jump scares! Sudden changes freak me out, especially changes in temperature. Please don't put me near a vent, radiator, or drafty window!

Aloe Vera

ALOE VERA

LIGHT: BRIGHT + INDIRECT
WATER: LOW
HUMIDITY: LOW TO HIGH
TEMPERATURE: AVERAGE TO HIGH
DIFFICULTY: 1

ORIGINALLY FROM THE ARABIAN PENINSULA. Hey, that windowsill of yours is looking a little empty. How about I post up there and we can get lit?! I don't mean partying (although my spiky leaves do look really fun). I mean I need a lot of indirect sunlight to survive. Fortunately, that's really all I need! I don't require much watering and you don't have to worry about fertilizer. I just want you to be the light of my life.

My ex would say

We had a toxic relationship. My leaves are toxic when consumed raw by people and pets. But what I lack in edibility, I make up for in healing properties. My leaves are famous for their soothing gel, which can be used on mild sunburn to help with itching and stinging. Here's a hot tip . . . uh, I mean, cold tip: Pop me in the fridge for a few minutes, then snap off a leaf to get extra-cool refreshing gel.

I have a reputation for

Being a late bloomer. Although I can bloom with spiky flowers in the right conditions, it will take many years and might not happen at all. If you're looking for a bunch of colorful blooms, try a florist.

My favorite time of year is

Cuffing season. Are you looking for someone to settle down with when it's cold out? I'm dormant in winter and rarely need to be watered in the frosty months. It's a perfect time to simply enjoy the pleasure of each other's company.

Mother of Thousands

KALANCHOE DAIGREMONTIANA

LIGHT: BRIGHT + INDIRECT
WATER: LOW + WELL-DRAINED
HUMIDITY: NORMAL TO HIGH
TEMPERATURE: AVERAGE
DIFFICULTY: 1

ORIGINALLY FROM MADAGASCAR. My name comes from the baby plantlets that sprout on my leaf edges, but I share a lot of other traits with moms, too: I'm hardy, patient, and I want to make your life easier. Do you want to be a co-parent with this low-maintenance succulent? Then call me Mommy!

My favorite holiday

Mother's Day, of course! When May comes around, consider gifting me a terracotta or clay pot. These help wick away moisture in my soil, which is great for a light drinker like me. (I only need to be watered every few weeks, and I don't appreciate soggy soil.)

Don't message me if

You're looking for a MILF (Mother I'd Like to Flower). Although I can grow small, tubular flowers when I'm planted outdoors in a warm environment, it's very rare for me to bloom as an indoor houseplant.

A trend I can't get behind

Hot yoga. Direct heat is a real mother of a problem for me. Although I can handle warmth, I don't like to be near heaters or heating vents. It dries out my leaves and my little plant babies. Think of the children!

Chinese Money Plant
PILEA PEPEROMIOIDES

LIGHT: AVERAGE TO BRIGHT + INDIRECT
WATER: REGULAR
HUMIDITY: NORMAL
TEMPERATURE: AVERAGE
DIFFICULTY: 2

ORIGINALLY FROM SOUTHERN CHINA. Craving something different? It's time to make a change. And like 2 of my many nicknames—Chinese Money Plant and Coin Plant—infer, I have plenty of spare change. I'm covered in coin-shaped leaves! With regular watering and good sunlight, my quirky appearance will add flair to any part of your home.

The award I should be nominated for
Friendliest. Like I said, I've got a ton of nicknames, which include Sharing Plant and Friendship Plant. I grow offshoots easily, and they're a cinch to propagate, so you can share the wealth!

I'm not afraid to
Show you how I'm feeling. I wear my feelings on my leaves, which can let you know what I need. If they curl up and brown along the edges, I'm probably not getting enough bright, indirect light or the room is too warm and too dry. If my leaves turn yellow and fall off, it's a sign that you're overwatering me.

My karaoke song is
"You Spin Me Round (Like a Record)" by Dead or Alive. (Trust me, you've heard this one!) Obviously, I'm a well-rounded individual—I mean, I'm literally made up of circles—but let this also serve as a reminder that you should rotate me regularly to keep my appearance even and symmetrical.

Polka Dot Begonia

BEGONIA MACULATA

LIGHT: BRIGHT + INDIRECT
WATER: REGULAR TO HIGH + WELL-DRAINED
HUMIDITY: NORMAL
TEMPERATURE: AVERAGE
DIFFICULTY: 3

ORIGINALLY FROM SOUTH AMERICA. Did I just catch you checking me out? You probably spotted my spots and became intrigued. I don't blame you. It's hard to look away from my white-speckled winglike leaves. (And, might I say, you have excellent taste.) Let's get to know each other and start connecting the dots.

I bring new meaning to the phrase

Being two-faced. It's not what you think! My leaves are dark green on top and the undersides are a rich orange-red. The pop of color is just part of my unique style!

You'll have to get used to

Me being picky. As a tropical plant, I have pretty specific needs, like an appropriate amount of water, steady humidity and temperature, and a soil refresh as I grow. My leaves will turn from green to yellow or brown as an indicator of insufficient care.

My must-have accessory

Small, sharp scissors. I can get a little leggy from reaching toward the sun if I don't get enough light. To keep me nice and bushy, prune a bit off my top a couple times a year. This will teach me to grow out, not up!

Triostar Stromanthe

STROMANTHE SANGUINEA

LIGHT: BRIGHT + INDIRECT
WATER: REGULAR
HUMIDITY: HIGH
TEMPERATURE: AVERAGE TO HIGH
DIFFICULTY: 3

ORIGINALLY FROM SOUTH AMERICA. HI THERE! IT'S REALLY NICE TO MEET YOU. WHAT'S THAT? OH, SORRY FOR RAISING MY VOICE, BUT IT'S PRETTY LOUD IN HERE . . . My big, bright leaves are pink, green, and fabulous, and they can really turn up the volume in any space.

A trend I can't get behind

Minimalism. Seriously, what's up with white and beige and blah? If you're a maximalist who loves color and flair, we'll get along really well. Just make sure I'm getting enough bright, indirect light so my variegation stays at its peak.

I can be a bit

Temperamental. If I'm not getting the exact care I need, I get pouty and my leaves will turn brown or yellow. If you give me too much water, I'll need some time to get over it. I might look sad and despondent for a few weeks, but we can work through it if you're patient.

This year, I really want to

Turn things around. Every week, please rotate my pot so I get an even amount of light. My leaves grow toward the sun, so my shape can get lopsided if you don't spin me regularly.

A deal breaker

Night owls. I'm a showstopper during the day, but as a prayer plant, my leaves move upward and fold together like hands praying when it's time for bed.

Sky Plant

TILLANDSIA IONANTHA

LIGHT: BRIGHT + INDIRECT
WATER: LOW
HUMIDITY: NORMAL TO HIGH
TEMPERATURE: LOW TO HIGH
DIFFICULTY: 1

ORIGINALLY FROM CENTRAL AND SOUTH AMERICA. Look! Up in the sky! It's not a bird, a plane, or even Superman. It's just me! I do have a pretty cool superpower, though: As an epiphyte, I don't need potting soil. So I'm the perfect plant if you don't like to get your hands dirty.

Three words to describe me

Small but mighty! I may be little, but I'm very adaptable, tough, and don't need a ton of maintenance.

Never have I ever

Found a room I couldn't thrive in. I can grow on tree branches and other plants, or you can put me in a glass terrarium, hang me from custom wire frames, stick me on a piece of decorative wood . . . I can bring my fun vibe anywhere.

We'll get along if

You like trying new things. Don't water me the old-fashioned way. Instead, soak me in room temperature water once a week for at least half an hour and give me a good misting every so often. When I'm fully hydrated, my leaves will feel stiff, not rubbery.

Money Tree

PACHIRA AQUATICA

LIGHT: BRIGHT + INDIRECT
WATER: HIGH
HUMIDITY: HIGH
TEMPERATURE: AVERAGE
DIFFICULTY: 2

ORIGINALLY FROM CENTRAL AND SOUTH AMERICA. They say money doesn't grow on trees, but you'll definitely want to invest in me. I'm a high-value houseplant that passes the vibe check—literally. In the practice of feng shui, I'm believed to bring positive energy and good fortune. That's why you often see me in banks and offices. I'm kind of like a finance bro at a successful hedge fund. (That pun was as intentional as my expensive intentions for you.)

My ideal first date
Let's go for a spin. I don't drive a car, but I love to be rotated monthly to keep my growth steady and even.

If I were a drink I'd be
Any cocktail with a twist. It pairs nicely with my trunks, which can be twisted together to make a braid.

You'll have to get used to
My heavy drinking. I'm a thirsty guy who likes to be watered frequently and regularly. I need a refill when the top of my soil runs dry, and you'd be the love of my life if you mist my leaves on the reg, too. This might sound a little demanding, but once you get the hang of our routine, you'll find I'm reliable and predictable.

My favorite song is
"B*tch Better Have My Money" by Rihanna.
(Told you I was predictable.)

Silver Bracts

PACHYPHYTUM BRACTEOSUM

LIGHT: BRIGHT
WATER: LOW
HUMIDITY: NORMAL
TEMPERATURE: AVERAGE
DIFFICULTY: 2

ORIGINALLY FROM MEXICO. If you're attracted to the thicc and curvy, then please allow me to introduce myself! I certainly live up to my scientific name (*Pachyphytum* is Latin for "thick") with my fleshy, succulent leaves that grow in chubby rosettes.

Something you can't tell by my photos
A lot of people's photos are so heavily edited these days, you might think I'm using a beauty filter. But this flawless finish is all natural, baby! I'm covered in a powdery coating of farina—a substance that protects my skin, while also giving me a soft, pastel look.

Biggest turn-off
I get the ick when water touches my leaves—it can even cause them to rot (like I said, ick!). My powdery makeup is not waterproof, so when you water me, which you won't have to do often, pour it straight onto my soil.

My motto is
Fun in the sun! Some people spend hours a day staring at a glowing screen, and I can relate. I need to spend about 6 hours every day staring at the glowing sun. Bright light helps me thrive, so I'd love for you to keep me in a south-facing window.

My favorite music is
Hard rock! In the wild, you can usually find me growing on rocks.

Maranta Lemon Lime

MARANTA LEUCONEURA 'LEMON LIME'

LIGHT: LOW TO BRIGHT + INDIRECT

WATER: HIGH

HUMIDITY: HIGH

TEMPERATURE: AVERAGE TO HIGH

DIFFICULTY: 2

ORIGINALLY FROM SOUTH AMERICA. I'm looking for someone to take me out to drinks and dinner—in that order. Since I'm from the tropics, I thrive in most conditions but only like to eat about once a month (an indoor-plant fertilizer does the trick).

You should not message me if
You're ready for a long-term commitment. While
I can be kept as a houseplant, I'm a slow grower
that doesn't have a great track record for longevity.
I'm here for a good time, not a long time!

My best party trick is
I'm a prayer plant—this common name comes from the
way my leaves fold up like praying hands. I do this at night
to preserve water, but throughout the day you'll be able
to worship my vividly patterned, decorative foliage.

My theme song is
"Like a Prayer" by Madonna

Philodendron Brasil

PHILODENDRON HEDERACEUM 'BRASIL'

LIGHT: LOW TO BRIGHT + INDIRECT
WATER: REGULAR + WELL-DRAINED
HUMIDITY: NORMAL TO HIGH
TEMPERATURE: LOW TO AVERAGE TO HIGH
DIFFICULTY: 1

ORIGINALLY FROM SOUTH AMERICA. *Olá!* If you're looking for a great hang that can turn into something more long term, stop swiping. I'm your match—an incredibly easy plant partner with zero chill. Consistent light and watering are enough to drive me up the wall with love.

My best feature

My flashy leaves! My two-tone variegation against my deep green leaves resembles the Brazilian flag (hence the name) and makes any space pop with the vibrant energy of Rio's Carnaval. To encourage fuller growth and larger leaves, prune any unruly vines during my active growing seasons in the spring or summer.

Never have I ever

I might be all over social media (#philodendron is one of the most popular trending houseplants), but I'm not into posting thirst traps. Too much water isn't good for me. Make sure you let my soil dry out between waterings.

I need a partner who

Isn't a big drinker—or understands that I'm not. I'm super sensitive to overwatering, and I'm prone to root rot. If my leaves start to yellow, all you need to do is cut back on the H_2O, and I'll feel better in no time.

Ponytail Palm
BEAUCARNEA RECURVATA

LIGHT: BRIGHT + DIRECT
WATER: LOW TO REGULAR
HUMIDITY: LOW
TEMPERATURE: AVERAGE
DIFFICULTY: 2

ORIGINALLY FROM MEXICO. I know we just met, but I'm ready for you to take me home! If you think things are moving too fast, don't worry—it takes me years and years to grow, so we can take things slow. (I'm not a grower, I'm a shower.) Even though I'm a tall tree when I'm planted outdoors, I'll be your petite pal when I'm living in your space.

You'd be surprised to learn
I'm not really a palm tree, but don't hold the lie against me! I'm actually a plant in the asparagus family. Perhaps you've met my edible cousin in the produce section? Anyway, you're lucky I'm not a real palm. Have you ever lived with one? I don't mean to throw shade (even though my long leaves are good at that), but they're really high maintenance and fussy. All I need is enough light and enough water.

My motto is
"Long hair don't care." My signature hairstyle is made up of long, leafy ribbons and I'm mostly carefree when it comes to upkeep.

Biggest turn-off
Inconsistency. Everyone knows that consistency is key in any relationship. I'm fairly low maintenance, but I still have standards! Although I don't need much to thrive, we'll both be happiest if I'm watered every 1 to 2 weeks and monthly in the winter.

ZZ Plant

ZAMIOCULCAS ZAMIIFOLIA

LIGHT: LOW TO BRIGHT + INDIRECT
WATER: LOW
HUMIDITY: LOW
TEMPERATURE: AVERAGE TO HIGH
DIFFICULTY: 1

ORIGINALLY FROM WEST TO SOUTH AFRICA. Around town, I'm known by many names: Zuzu Plant, Eternity Plant, Aroid Palm, Zanzibar Gem. But only the real ones can pronounce my name correctly. Zam-ee-oh-kul-kass zam-ee-foh-lee-uh. Actually, you know what? ZZ is good.

My ex would say
I'm a breath of fresh air. In return for keeping me alive, I'll actually purify the air of whatever room I'm in. However, I am toxic to pets, so just keep me out of their reach.

Something you can't tell by my photos
I'm a triplet. My fraternal siblings are the Raven ZZ, who's soft and green when it starts growing but hardens to a glossy black and the Variegated ZZ, with cream and green leaves. They might be the more colorful members of the family, but we're all hardy and easygoing.

Don't hate me if
I ignore your thirst traps. Just below the soil my rhizomes, or bulbous stems, "swell" to store water. Hope you don't mind, but they make me pretty self-sufficient. #neverthirsty

Bromeliad

BROMELIACEAE

LIGHT: AVERAGE TO BRIGHT + INDIRECT
WATER: REGULAR + WELL-DRAINED
HUMIDITY: NORMAL TO HIGH
TEMPERATURE: AVERAGE TO HIGH
DIFFICULTY: 2

ORIGINALLY FROM TROPICAL PARTS OF THE AMERICAS. You can google me before we meet, but if you're looking for dirt, you're not going to dig up much. That's because I'm planted in shallow soil. There are many different varieties of bromeliads (see the Sky Plant on page 86), and we're all epiphytes, or air plants, so we can grow without soil. The only "stalking" that's relevant here is the stalk of my flashy flower.

My ex would say

I'm a bit clingy. I'm known to cling to trees, and if you keep me in your home as an air plant without soil, I need to be affixed to an object or kept in a sturdy vessel. To water me, soak me in room temperature water for at least half an hour once a week or when my leaves feel rubbery.

One thing I'll never do again

Bloom. I only flower once during my lifespan, and only in the right conditions. Like many great loves, I'm once in a lifetime.

My ideal first date

Let's have a family-style meal or go to a tapas restaurant. I love to mix things up when I'm eating. When I'm potted, I go for a mix of soil and sand. You can also give me charcoal, orchid mix, or a soil-free potting mix.

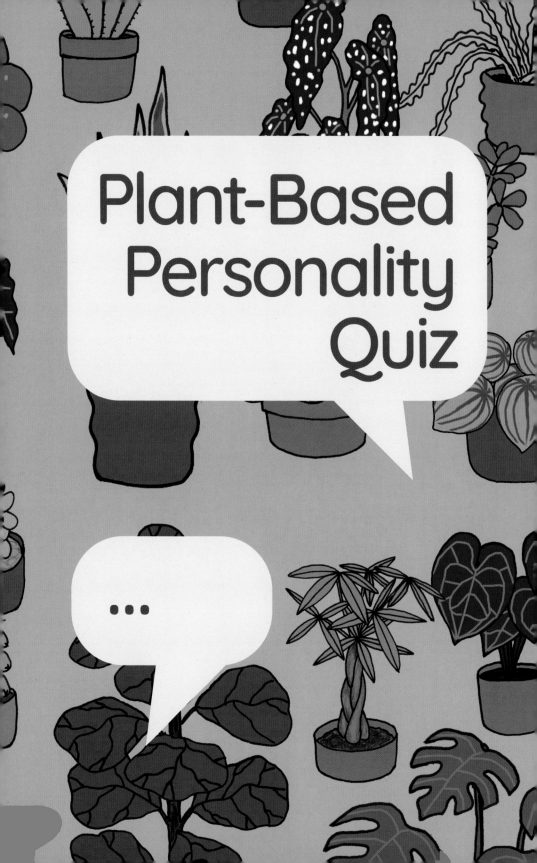

Not sure where to start on your plant-based dating journey? Take this compatibility quiz to find an unbe*leafable* houseplant that suits you and your lifestyle.

1. How do you like to celebrate your birthday?

   a A rager, an afterparty, and a hangover brunch the next day

   b A low-key dinner with your ride-or-dies

   c A weekend getaway with your lover

   d Happy hour drinks with coworkers

   e Hosting a fundraiser for your favorite nonprofit

2. You're craving a snack. What do you eat?

   a An over-the-top cupcake from a trendy bakery

   b Whatever you can find in the fridge

   c Leftovers from a homecooked meal

   d Free snacks from the office kitchen

   e Carrot sticks and hummus

3. What are you bingeing on Netflix?

   a An obscure independent film

   b Reruns of a favorite show while you scroll through your phone

   c A long-running series you never want to end

   d A reality competition that showcases entrepreneurial talent

   e A wildlife documentary that highlights conservation efforts

4. What's your biggest turn-off?

   a Someone who isn't adventurous

   b Someone who is too clingy

   c Someone who is afraid of commitment

   d Someone who isn't career- and goals-focused

   e Someone who doesn't recycle

5. You're redecorating your room. Pick a style.

a Maximalism, baby! Accent walls and patterned wallpaper!

b I never stay in one place long enough to decorate.

c A cozy love nest full of DIYs

d A hybrid space for work and rest

e Sustainable with your favorite thrift store finds

6. How would you like to spend your next vacation?

a Partying in Miami, NYC, and Ibiza—in that order

b A solo camping trip in Joshua Tree

c A cozy cabin with friends—you have the whole menu planned

d Anywhere with good WiFi so you can check work emails

e An ocean cleanup retreat in Costa Rica

7. Your best friend would describe you as

a The baddest B in the game

b Flaky and noncommittal

c A serial monogamist

d A serial entrepreneur and workaholic

e Crunchy-granola

8. Which animal do you identify with?

a Rainbow glitter unicorn

b Lone wolf

c Mother hen

d Worker bee

e Peaceful dove

9. Describe your ideal wedding.

a A huge celebration with everyone you've ever met

b An elopement in Vegas that can be easily annulled

c A traditional ceremony at your childhood church

d One that's planned by someone else

e A beachside exchange of vows

10. What's your dream job?

a A party planner

b Consulting and freelance gigs so I can make my own schedule

c A nurse

d The CEO of a Fortune 500 company

e A spiritual healer

MOSTLY AS
Power Couple
You're not afraid to stand out, so you should have a powerful plant that complements your flashy flair. Consider a plant that makes a statement, like a monstera (page 37), pink princess philodendron (page 73), or a bird of paradise (page 45).

MOSTLY BS
Casual Fling
You value your independence and you're not looking for anything too serious. You've got more of a numb thumb than a green thumb, so you're best suited to a snake plant (page 34) or ZZ plant (page 98). These plants are easy, undemanding, and don't need constant attention.

MOSTLY CS:
Nature Nurturer
You've got a lot of love to give and you're looking for a plant that will appreciate your doting affection. A polka dot begonia (page 82), triostar stromanthe (page 85), and calathea orbifolia (page 38) need a lot of care and are rewarding for nurturers.

MOSTLY DS
Office Romance
Your motto is "rise and grind" and you're always hustling at work. Don't let that stop you from getting a leafy companion! There are plenty of small plants that are suited to low-light office spaces, including a sky plant (page 86), boobie cactus (page 49) and money tree (page 89).

MOSTLY ES:
Clean Living
You're a sustainably minded, health-conscious person who doesn't want anything toxic in your life—not in your food, not in your relationships, and certainly not in your home. Some plants with air-purifying to cleanse your space include: pothos (pages 46 and 62), rubber tree (page 41), and spider plant (page 42).

Quick & Dirty Index

Difficulty

Low-Maintenance

LOW LIGHT
Bird of Paradise (page 45)
Boobie Cactus (page 49)
Cebu Blue (page 62)
Golden Pothos (page 46)
Hindu Rope Plant (page 74)
Maranta Lemon Lime
  (page 93)
Philodendron Brasil (page 94)
Pink Princess Philodendron
  (page 73)
Round-Leaf Calathea
  (page 38)
Snake Plant (page 34)
Spider Plant (page 42)
Watermelon Peperomia
  (page 53)
ZZ Plant (page 98)

LOW WATER
Aloe Vera (page 77)
Boobie Cactus (page 49)
Hindu Rope Plant (page 74)
Mother of Thousands
  (page 78)
Ponytail Palm (page 97)
Silver Bracts (page 90)
Sky Plant (page 86)
Snake Plant (page 34)
String of Pearls (page 66)
Sweetheart Plant (page 69)
ZZ Plant (page 98)

Size

BIG
Bird of Paradise (page 45)
Fiddle-Leaf Fig (page 54)
Monstera Deliciosa (page 37)
Rubber Tree (page 41)

SMALL
Aloe Vera (page 77)
Boobie Cactus (page 49)
Jade Plant (page 57)
Silver Bracts (page 90)
Sky Plant (page 86)
Sweetheart Plant (page 69

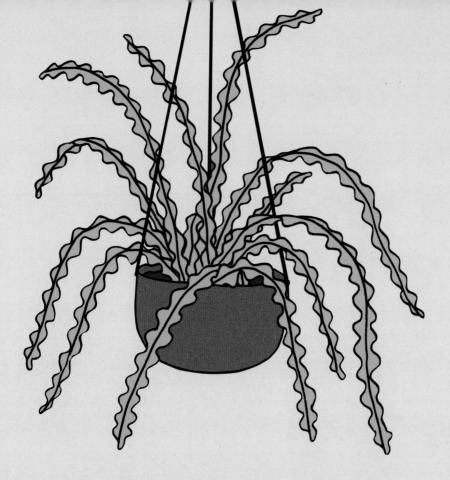

Pet-Friendly

Good for Hanging

Flowering

Showstoppers

ABOUT THE AUTHOR

Agatha Isabel is a bad b*tch. After moving to Brooklyn from LA, she began her plant collection and rediscovered a deep connection with nature. She's passionate about community-building in all aspects of her life, and through Planting for Progress, a community-sourced project that raised money for human rights and local organizations, and her shop, Plant Ma, she has created a thriving plant community. With nature as her muse, she writes, paints, and travels to tropical locations as a creative outlet to balance her professional tech and privacy career. She can usually be found volunteering with local nonprofits, exploring new nature spots, vibing at a concert, or trying to find love on a dating app. She is currently based in Southern California.

Find her on www.agathaisabel.com.

ABOUT THE ILLUSTRATOR

Mai Ly Degnan is an award-winning illustrator, currently based in Baltimore, MD. Her work consists of bright colors, patterned details, tedious linework, and playfully stylized characters. She enjoys creating "slice of life" illustrations that celebrate everyday people in their day-to-day. When she isn't freelancing, she also works as a full-time professor, teaching in the illustration practice MFA program at the Maryland Institute College of Art.

Her work has been recognized by the Society of Illustrators of New York and Los Angeles, *American Illustration*, and *3x3*. Selected clients include Huffington Post, Quarto Kids, Alba Editorial, *Cosmopolitan* UK, the Norman Rockwell Museum, the *Boston Globe*, *Time* magazine, Harper Collins, NPR, *VICE* magazine, Magic Cat Publishing, and others.